H45 547 303 8

942 BET
07/12.

D1381052

Please renew/return items by last date
shown. Please call the number below:

Renewals and enquiries:     0300 123 4049

Textphone for hearing or
speech impaired users:      0300 123 4041

www.hertsdirect.org/librarycatalogue
L32

Hertfordshire

# WRITERS' BRITAIN

# ENGLISH CITIES

### AND

# SMALL TOWNS

In the same series

# ENGLISH CITIES
## AND
# SMALL TOWNS

JOHN BETJEMAN

*with*
*8 plates in colour*
*and*
*25 illustrations in*
*black & white*

PRION

This edition published in Great Britain by Prion
32-34 Gordon House Road
London NW5 1LP

Text copyright © 1943 the Estate of John Betjeman
This compilation copyright © Prion 1997

First published in 1943 by Collins

A catalogue record of this book can be obtained
from the British Library

ISBN 1-85375-251-7

Colour origination by MRM Graphics, Singapore
Printed and bound in Singapore

# UNDER THE MICROSCOPE

Cities and towns, the various haunts of men
Require the pencil; they defy the pen:
Could he, who sung so well the Grecian fleet,
So well have sung of alley, lane or street?
Can measured lines these various buildings show,
The Town Hall Turning, or the Prospect Row?
Can I the seats of wealth and want explore
And lengthen out my lays from door to door?

*Rev. George Crabbe*: THE BOROUGH

NOT UNTIL YOU HAVE BEEN AWAY FROM IT, AS HAS
the author of this book for more than a year, do
you realise how friendly, how beautiful is the meanest
English town. Not the most magnificent scenery, misty
mountains, raging seas, desert sunsets, or groves of
orange can compensate for the loss of the Corn
Exchange, the doctor's house, tennis in suburban gardens, the bank and the bank-manager's house, the rural

SOUTH GATE STREET, LEICESTER
Colour engraving by I. Flower. *c.* 1820

garages, the arid municipal park, the church clock and the Jubilee drinking fountain. Even a town like Wolverhampton looks splendid through Memory's telescope, while tears of homesickness blur the focus of Blandford's market square and the grey, shut-in climb of Bodmin's main street. Sitting here, remembering the provincial towns of England, I wonder why it is that they hold me, as they do thousands of my countrymen, with a spell that not all their obvious faults can break. Their harmony and proportion were frequently damaged (far more effectively than they have been since by bombs) by modernistic shop fronts, pretentious gleaming buildings and enormous cinemas: they are girded about with semi-detached villas: they have been chopped into and straightened out for the convenience of motorists who gave them hardly a glance as they roared through them in those days of no time and too much petrol, before this war started. Why is it then, that they are so attractive?

Possibly it is because English people who live in towns retain the country talent for gardening. Where there is no garden, back or front, wherein to plant flowers (now vegetables) there is a window box. Thus it is that the country seems to creep right into the town, growing more defiant as it thins. Possibly, too, the visitor finds himself sharing, unconsciously the local pride in the place. Though few people in England are borough-conscious (with a sense of loyalty to an area demarcated by some Municipal Reform Act of the late nineteenth century) most inhabitants of towns of all sizes have an immense pride in the place from the earliest doorway to the latest bomb crater.

When exploring, for the first time, one of these pockets of English history, local pride and marked character, the approach I like to make is by railway, for from the railway line you get an impression of the surrounding country, undisturbed by the adjuncts of a main road. The space before the station is lined first by a row of once successful shops, now less successful as the station has come to be less used. A road cuts for a few hundred yards through new brick villas to the heart of the old town. This road is probably called 'Station Row,' the name in white on a blue tin background affixed to the bright red wall of the side of a house. The villas are of a type not later than 1910, for few railway stations were built after that date; they are two-storeyed, probably bow-fronted and may be relieved here and there with white brick dressings and varieties of stained glass in the panels of the front door. They each have trim little gardens with privet hedges and squeaking cast iron gates painted green or plum. An aid to the date of those villas may be gleaned from the names, generally written on the glass pane above the hall door: memories of the Crimea, the Indian

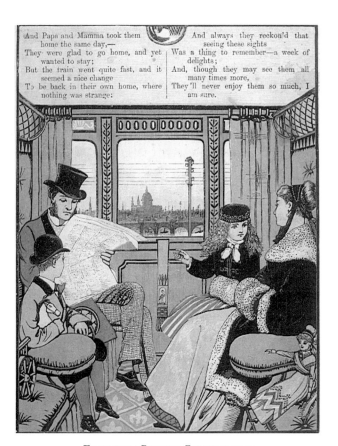

And Papa and Mamma took them
  home the same day,—
They were glad to go home, and yet
  wanted to stay;
But the train went quite fast, and it
  seemed a nice change
To be back in their own home, where
  nothing was strange:

And always they reckon'd that
  seeing these sights
Was a thing to remember—a week of
  delights;
And, though they may see them all
  many times more,
They'll never enjoy them so much, I
  am sure.

FAMILY IN A RAILWAY COMPARTMENT
Illustration by Thomas Crane, *c.* 1885

Mutiny, the Jubilee or the Boer wars, basking in varieties of signwriter's lettering on gate, pillar and panel.

On reaching the High Street or Market Place, I use considerable discretion about the choice of an hotel. Many a thoughtless motorist has been taken in by new paint on the exterior or a wealth of half timber or a reference in a road book. Personally I always prefer rather seedy exteriors; a house which is not owned by a chain of hotels—places with the words 'Family and Commercial' outside, and lace curtains giving a vista of brown wallpaper, a mahogany sideboard, bottles of H.P. Sauce and steel engravings. Here there are usually feather beds, a hot water bottle and a lively trade in the bar with local men.

My next step is to take a walk to the biggest stationers and consult one of the revolving stands of views; there I generally find postcards, taken by a local photographer, of the country houses in the neighbourhood, the war memorial, the Cottage Hospital, the High Street, the Parish Church exterior and interior and who knows but that among them might not be a view of some old custom held annually in the town or of a cavern with stalactites, a 'folly' in a park, a medicinal spring, or some other local matter of interest which would escape the casual visitor. I also buy a local guide. This may take the form of one published by a distant firm and paid for by the advertisements of which it mostly consists, of the

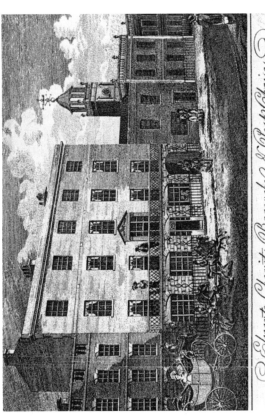

THE HEN AND CHICKENS HOTEL, BIRMINGHAM
Nineteenth-century advertisement

town's tradesmen, or if the stationer, as so often is the case, was also a printer, it might be written and printed in the town itself. In either case it will contain nothing but praise about everything in the place from the very scanty remains of a Norman castle by the river, to the red and brown terracotta frontage of the Town Hall. It will also tell me of any prominent person born in the town or connected with it and this may be someone so totally unexpected as Robert Browning or Captain Webb or Lillywhite. At the local stationers, too, may be a book by a local author of talent wedged in between the limp leather editions of Ella Wheeler Wilcox. Nor will I forget to buy the local newspaper and soak myself in neighbouring parish news and rows of the district council.

Round the parish church are narrow alleys and similar alleys lead off the High Street. These are the oldest parts of the town, the relics of the age of carts and country fairs. If there is light I would walk back from the stationers to the hotel by these alleys with the aid of the map in the guide book. They run the length of the garden of a town house, lilacs appear over the high brick wall and beyond them can be heard the twang of a tennis racket in the evening as the bank manager's children go on for as long as the light lasts. One side of the passage is garden wall, the other is cottages, small, squalid, red brick, built in the days of

Chartists on the back garden of a house in the High Street for a century now given over entirely to commerce. And turning round I am able to survey the backs of the houses in the High Street. These are often most informative: steep gables appear with leaded windows of the seventeenth century; another house is hung with tiles arranged in patterns, another reveals timber construction of a sixteenth century cottage on to which an imposing house has been built to face the High Street in the late Georgian period; another house, dull enough on the High Street front when it was faced with terracotta by the shopkeeper who owned it, so as to be in line with the 1880-Renaissance of the Town Hall, reveals itself at the back as a handsome Georgian town house with a bow window, a neat brick elevation, the panes of brown glass in whose windows reflect here and there scooped hollows of late sunlight. Newbury is a town in which the side lanes take you straight from the twentieth century to the eighteenth. But every old town of England has these alleys which suddenly reveal how once the place must have appeared. Out again in the High Street I watch the upper storeys of the houses, above the shops, where here and there a Venetian window or a bow window with a delicate iron balcony or an old gabled house emerges from the Commerce at its feet. The shops too are a pleasure. Chemists shops in provincial towns have

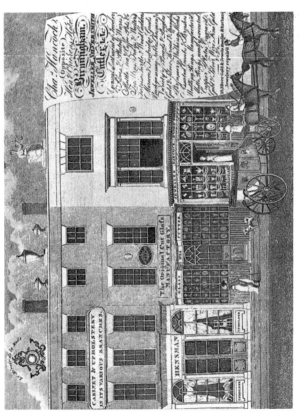

HANCOCK'S GLASS SHOP, BIRMINGHAM
Nineteenth-century advertisement

often preserved the dignified and convenient interiors of the early Victorian era—rows of little wooden drawers with the names of their contents in black lettering on a gold background, above them old round jars with similar lettering and in the window the big coloured glass bottles of the last century Here and there in a poor quarter of the town there may be one or two old shop fronts with the square panes and bowed front and neat carving around the door and across the fascia. Personally I most enjoy the atmosphere of the town's emporium where there are those elevated railways running from various counters to the cash desk and where incandescent gas blooms amid brass rods suspending underwear and curtain fabrics.

In the Hotel, with the aid of Kelly's Directory—there is generally an old edition in the Commercial Room—and the plan of the town in the local guide, I have a pleasant evening working out the history, situation and architecture of the place. The best guide books of all are old ones published in the last century, Black's, Murray's, etc., but these are not always easy to get; the next best is Kelly's Directory. I have never understood why this painstaking firm does not publish a separate volume of the descriptive information it gives at the head of each place in its county directories. From Kelly, which has a thorough and uncritical account of the town, I learn that its streets are lighted by gas, that it returned two members to Parliament until the Reform Bill, that the branch railway was opened in 1875 (thus confirming the date of the houses in Station Row) that the Parish Church was restored in 1860, again in 1875 when a new chancel was added, that the Town Hall was built in 1887, that there is a rope factory at Brick End and that there is a market on Tuesday, that the subsoil is gravel, that the brickfields are now disused, besides a heap of other information which the average guide book with its bias in favour of what is fragmentary and 'ancient' (pre-1700) omits altogether. For instance, I read that there is a Unitarian Church built in 1776. This will be worth going to see. On the following morning after a considerable effort to find the key, the old oak door of a modest brick chapel reveals an interior of box pews, high pulpit, clear glass windows and Chippendale Communion Table, untouched since the days when black-gowned preachers thundered against Arminius or Calvin, and godly souls drank in their instructions while children watched the bluebottles crawling up the sunny glass window, over the top of the pew. It is a mistake to suppose that in a country town the old parish church is always the most ancient building. Alas, too often it has been sumptuously restored in the last century to which the taste of the present for powder blue hangings, Margaret Tarrant pictures in the 'Children's Corner' and

The Boston May Sheep Fair, 1830

L. Burleigh Bruhl

THAXTED, ESSEX, THE MANOR HALL.

unstained oak 'kneelers' has been added, so that little beyond the proportions of the old interior remains. Only by worshipping in the church, at an early Communion service, do I forget the restoration and learn to love the building. The outside may be fine and there may be a photograph of the interior before 'restoration' in the vestry. But the nonconformist chapels, especially those belonging to Unitarians, Moravians, Quakers and Congregationalists, Baptists and Methodists are worth seeing, outside at any rate. Up to 1840, they are graceful; later than that they are often strikingly original—more so than the dull copying restoration of the buildings of the Establishment. If the town is large enough for a 'chapel of ease' to the Parish Church, this will probably be worth seeing and Kelly will give the name of the architect. If it be Street, Seddon, Pearson, Brookes, Ferrey, Blomfield, Scott, or if it appears to have cost a lot of money (Kelly often gives the cost) you may count on finding an imposing Victorian building, of bold proportions and with good carved stonework. It will probably have been built either (1) as a result of a row between the High Church members of the parish church congregation who found that place of worship too 'low' or (2) the reverse or (3) as a mission to the poorer part of the town fired by the readers of the excellent novels of Charlotte M. Yonge in the latter half of the nineteenth century when the social conscience of the Established Church awoke to vigour. Besides the buildings there is the local museum. Here, there are sure to be water colours of the place done in the early nineteenth century) when almost anyone of sensibility who put brush to paper was able to catch the atmosphere of what must have been the most beautiful town architecture in the world. If there is no museum there are generally some old water colours and topo-graphical oil paintings hanging in the Town Hall. The Corn Exchange, the Assize Court and the local Doctor's house will also be worth a visit. For some reason Doctors and Solicitors manage to inhabit the most imposing Georgian houses in a small town and often enough these houses have carved oak staircases, of the eighteenth century, ceilings with plaster cherubs and marble mantelpieces and panelled rooms. East Anglia, Wilts, Dorset and Salop are particularly rich in them.

The architectural part of the investigation, prepared from Kelly and the local map, is not quite completed. On the inner outskirts of the town there is a row of houses called Albemarle Villas or Clarence Crescent or Nelson Square, indicative of the late Georgian era, the time of George III and his sons, of spas and watering places. Here you may find that greatest British contribution to architecture after the Perpendicular style, the austere Georgian stucco villa of proportions so subtle—tall oblong windows with thin wooden glazing bars on the

Newbury, Berkshire, 1920

ground floor, square windows some distance along and broad eaves, low pitched slate roof and solid oblong chimney stacks—that it will fit into any landscape and enhance any colour with which its tenant may choose to wash the chaste exterior. Notice particularly the ironwork of the balcony and verandah and the fence around the square or shrubbery in front—if it has not been taken by over-zealous local authorities.

Sometimes I draw a blank, sometimes a name or a date in Kelly promises too much; but I can recollect no English town which is devoid of interest and if there are no old buildings to see, there is always pleasant entertainment to be got from the modern ones and instruction and friends to be found among the inhabitants. Soft, friendly welcome of the little book-lined study of the local antiquary ! Narrow hall, with tea and warm fire below the marble mantelpiece, ticking presentation clock and yellowing collection of photographs! Shelves of local poets and green bound proceedings of the County Archaeological Society! Cold wide hall of the rectory, brown theological shelves in the Rector's study, College group and ordination portrait, college crest and maybe, college oar! Sweet shyness of the rector's youngest daughter by the little wicket gate across the lawn. The church tower among the trees! How often have I had tea and talk with friendly rectors and walked back through winding streets or out to where the newest houses meet the country. Then what a pleasure it is to speculate on how he made his money who built yonder semi-Tudor villa, planted that rock garden, stuck with stone enough to fill a cemetery; to gaze through into front rooms where the inevitable sideboard looking-glass reflects the biscuit barrel and the street again. Or in the morning, what pleasant suburban sights meet my eye as I walk to the station bound for some other town. I am reminded of that moving passage about a provincial suburb in Gissing's story *Fate and the Apothecary* describing, I think it must be, an outskirt of Exeter:

'Farmiloe. Chemist by Examination.' So did the good man proclaim himself to a suburb of a city in the West of England. It was one of those pretty, clean, fresh-coloured suburbs only to be found in the west; a few dainty little shops, everything about them bright or glistening, scattered among pleasant little houses with gardens eternally green and all but perennially in bloom; every vista ending in foliage and in one direction a far glimpse of the Cathedral towers, sending forth their music to fall dreamily upon these quiet roads. The neighbourhood seemed to breathe a tranquil prosperity. Red cheeked emissaries of butcher, baker and grocer, order books in hand, knocked cheerily at kitchen doors and went smiling away; the ponies were well fed and frisky, their carts spick and span. The church of the parish, an imposing edifice, dated only from a few years ago and had cost its noble founder a sum of money which any church-going parishioner would have named to you with proper awe. The population was largely female.

This describes late Victorian England, but the same scene exists in provincial towns to-day. Main roads have swept through the delicate textured high streets, cobbles have been replaced by tarmac and multiple stores have drained sedate old Oriental warehouses of their trade, garages have replaced the smithies, little smelly vans have ousted the pony carts; but still the suburb remains the sunny abode that Gissing knew; still of a workday, before the war, you could hear the bell of a muffin man and still of a Sunday, a good crowd came to choral matins in shining Victorian churches where pew rents were still paid and where visiting cards were still fixed in a little brass socket at the entrance to the pew.

Lastly come the various types of inn. Fake half timbering is very popular for cocktail bars of larger hotels, where it is a cheap and convenient method of turning a shed in the yard, formerly a scullery or pantry, into the semblance of what many people fondly imagine was Shakespeare's England. These big hotel bars, are almost always patronised by motorists, visitors, strangers and the richer stratum of the country

PUB IN CANNING TOWN,
Oil painting by Henry Lamb, 1928

town, not by the local people who prefer stone or tile floors, wooden benches, yellow wallpaper in imitation of grained wood, a framed advertisement for beer on the walls. This old type of inn interior is unpopular with brewers who like palms, little tables, stained glass and who discourage standing up against the bar. In many towns now, the least spoiled bars are those in the neighbourhood of the railway station, built at some expense in the Victorian era, with mahogany, engraved glass, brass fixtures and gas or electroliers, all in such a sumptuous durable material that the brewers have not had the heart to spoil them with refurnishing

# A CHOICE OF CATHEDRAL,
# UNIVERSITY AND COUNTRY
# TOWNS

IN SO SHORT A BOOK AS THIS I CANNOT DESCRIBE IN adequate detail even a single English town, among the many there are, as good as unnoticed by all save Kelly, which are worthy of the most searching description. In many of the larger towns, buildings have been destroyed by the Nazis and I might find myself describing a church or terrace or house which is now less than a shell. But no-one imagines that a building that has been shattered by bombs is irreparable. After the last war many of the Cathedrals and churches of Northern France were restored in such a way that the most trained eye could hardly detect when the rebuilding had occurred. Recent bombings have blown out a lot of very ugly stained glass, a long way after the pre-Raphaelites. Incendiaries have burned much unwelcome woodwork in churches which, for the last sixty years, have probably been little more than shells of their mediaeval or Georgian selves. Nor does a town disappear from bombing. My friend, Mr. John Piper, the

WYE BRIDGE AND CATHEDRAL, HEREFORD,
Water colour by Vincent Lines

war artist, who was sent to Bath to make a picture of the damage, writing to me says, 'I was miserable there indeed to see that haunt of ancient water-drinkers besmirched with dust and blast . . . But the air of Bath was still there and the back alleys and the raised voices in courtyards, only all talking about how they'd escaped . . . Bath will survive. Bombing does not destroy towns. They get even more of their own character to compensate.'

English Cathedrals are, most of them, larger than any other cathedrals in Europe, except St. Peter's. They are a memorial of the time when people referred to 'the pious English' and when the square mile of the City of London had over one hundred churches. And to this day, the presence of the church, symbolised by the Cathedral, broods over most cathedral towns. From the distance, whether the town is in a valley or on a hill top, the Cathedral rides above the houses and draws the landscape round it, flat East Anglian pasture or rounded chalk downs of Wiltshire. When you are in the town itself the Cathedral disappears, though its personality pervades the place in many little churches, some 'low,' some 'high,' some locked, some bombed, most hidden among shops and winding alleys. Gaitered archdeacons and frequent clergy of less distinctive dress, haunt the Cathedral café, the Cathedral bookshop, the Chauntrye tea shoppe, the Cloister antique shop. Then suddenly at the end of a street or through some monastic gateway to the Close you see the Cathedral soaring into the sky. At once it is bigger, more majestic, more richly textured than you would have believed possible. And in the silence of the Close, where ilex, lilac and copper beech hang over walled gardens of the Canons' houses and where gigantic elms rise from smooth stretches of emerald grass, the Cathedral is so vast and so old, so unbelievable a piece of engineering in the poise and counterpoise of local stone that you feel you must whisper, if you want to speak at all, even outside it.

Here in another country my mind goes to Salisbury, my favourite cathedral city. There is the usual wide market square of a county town, mellow brick houses and a quantity of inns, some small beer houses for thirsty drovers, some jazzed up hostelryes for motorists; there is St. Thomas's church, of pale grey stone among the red tiles and brick, with its slender fifteenth century interior: the main streets whose multiple stores have left fairly unharmed the old buildings above the shop fronts, the long grey wall of the Cathedral precincts, and then that huge, silent, tree-shadowed close, acres of retreating grass as a setting for the vertical lines of the great cathedral with its tremendous spire nearly as high as the distant downs.

And if the interior of Salisbury is now a little cold,

THE PEACE FESTIVAL AT SALISBURY, 1856
Lithograph by M. and N. Hanhart

stripped of its wall painting and ancient glass, I think of Winchester, that endless nave where screen and transept and aisle suggest, by branching roof and intersecting vaults, vista upon vista beyond to God himself. Or I remember an Evensong at Hereford, a remote Cathedral less visited than many, where I was one of a small congregation, listening to the contemplative service of Evensong which had been kept up through the Reformation and the centuries; the well-trained choir from the choir school, the tenors and basses and altos from the town: the psalms: a Canon reading the lesson, appearing from the dark recess of a stall: the intoned prayers and the 'Amen' floating up to the vaulting: the sweet Victorian anthem in tune with Sir Gilbert Scott's pious restoration of the fabric. Or I am back at a Three Choirs Festival in Gloucester, hearing Handel among the heavy Norman pillars of the Nave and glimpsing, beyond, that lace-like miracle of glass and stone, the Choir at Gloucester where England first bred the Perpendicular style, the last and, to me, most beautiful phase of Gothic. Or I am saying my last prayers in England, before leaving for Ireland, in the early light shining on pink sandstone in Chester Cathedral, a square and strong and Northern looking building. Or I am rowing on the river at Ely and glancing up at the Cathedral on the slope above me, the ingenious lantern at the intersection of nave transepts and choir,

ELY CATHEDRAL

Engraving from J. M. W. Turner's *Picturesque Views of England and Wales*, 1838

the stately towers at the west, the aisles and chapels bursting out from the masonry into rich churches of their own. Three other Cathedral memories remain: being shewn round Canterbury at midnight by the light of an electric torch on Norman capital and distant vault and finally there at my feet a circle of light on the spot where St. Thomas à Becket was murdered: standing in the whispering gallery of St. Paul's as the shadows grew down the empty nave on the night of one of the heaviest raids on the City when a time bomb fell into St. Paul's Churchyard and did not explode: a fine September evening in that first most sinister year of the War, when the Youth Fellowship of my home village was having its final fling, a day's outing by char-a-banc to Cheddar Gorge; the Bishop shewed us round the moated Palace at Wells and from the palace garden we looked across to the east end of the Cathedral where the late light cast long shadows on the golden Somerset stone. I remember thinking then that I must store in my mind every detail, the flowers in the palace garden, the fishponds, the sculptured proportions of that kind country cathedral, for here was the heart of England, and an unforgettable monument of Christendom.

However you see them, whether for a service, or for a moment in the close, or for a gaping, guide-conducted tour, the Cathedrals dwarf the towns and cities where they are. When you are out again in the streets, shops

THE CATHEDRAL, CHESTER

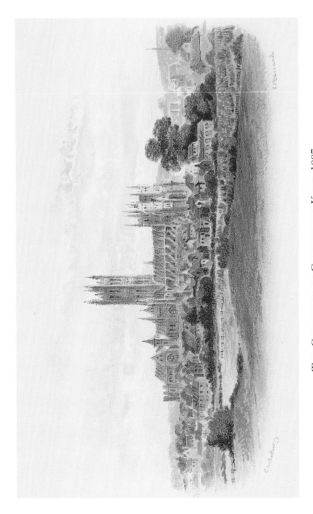

The Cathedral at Canterbury, Kent, 1887

and war and factories and buses and trams are trivial and unimportant. In some places, the town has become industrialised and eaten its way almost to the Cathedral gates as at Chester, Gloucester, Durham and Worcester, or it has hardly grown at all as at Ely and Wells; or it has become noisy and crowded, too narrow and old for all the traffic which has been allowed by a careless generation to pour into it, as at Chichester, York, Winchester, Salisbury and St. Albans: whatever has happened, the Cathedral still rules. Loud over the internal combustion engine sound its bells, even if, for the present, they only strike the hour.

And next to the Cathedral towns, come the University towns of Oxford and Cambridge, in my affection. Oxford, though it has a small Cathedral, comes first in the guide books, but second as a place of fine architecture. For Oxford is really three towns: at the heart of it is the University where the great Renaissance dome of the Radcliffe Library gathers round it neighbouring Gothic towers, where small gateways give on to large quadrangles, where Cotswold stone, flaked and ancient, goes purple in the rain and golden in the sunlight, where the High Street curves up from weeping willows at Magdalen Bridge and traffic thunders past the fronts of colleges, where bells sound at every quarter with such divergence from such a variety of towers and steeples as almost to make it seem that bells are ringing all the time; where wallflowers still grow on college walls as Newman saw them and dons in billowing gowns sweep under archways and bicycles abound. That is the University. Then there is the City, the place of Oxfordshire and Berkshire farmers and tradespeople, with a Castle, an Assize Court, two stations and a cattle market. Even without the University, it would be attractive enough like Wallingford or Abingdon or any other fair-sized country town. The third town is a modern industrial growth, with rows of modern villas, arcades of chain stores, elephantine cinemas and gleaming factories. It is some way off from its two old parents, but its people, its shops and its villas have encircled them and throttled their old throats.

For this reason Cambridge is now more beautiful than Oxford. It has been less industrialised. For me there is a personal affection for Oxford, but I can see that to the unbiased, the windy East Anglian town has a finer collection of buildings. The silver grey classic Senate House; the romantic screen on King's Parade to King's College Chapel; evening light in the chapel with the colours dying in that forest of Tudor stone and glass and the distant choir filing out of the candle light and high, high above us the complicated roof – not even Wordsworth's sonnet does justice to this most exquisite interior; early spring on the 'backs' with weeping willows and the grey colleges, the little balustered

HOUSES AT OXFORD
Water colour by George Pyne, c. 1800–1884

bridges of stone over the river, and behind them the airy, fanciful Gothic of St. John's and over all one of those great, windy skies that Tennyson loved; the market town and the diversity of college buildings, some silver stone, and some mellow brick: these all should make Cambridge not second but first in the next Baedeker.

Oxford and Cambridge stand somewhat apart, like the Cathedral towns. But how am I going to describe the three hundred and seventy quiet inland towns of England? Three times now, I have tried to write this part of the book. First I wrote of the show towns—Stratford-on-Avon, Ludlow, Rye and Winchelsea, Burford: then it seemed that I had left out those I ought to mention, more alive than the show places because less self-conscious and less well-known. Then I tried to mention all the small towns, however briefly, tried to fit into a few words the wind-swept, fortress-like North, brick and flint East Anglian towns, stony Cotswold places huddled among the sheep hills, rich West Country orchard towns, modest Midland boroughs—but the result was too condensed. I am at a loss. English country towns are all different: their pattern and their history is on the surface similar, but below it is full of individual character. Each has its now disrupting social scale of Big House, rector, solicitor, Mayor, shopkeeper, worker: each has its High Street or Market

King's College Chapel, from the backs, Cambridge

Water colour by Edward Vulliamy

Square where once a week or once a month the shops are open to a late hour, the little inns are full and cattle, carts and cars block the roads because it is market day: each is a capital in itself to neighbouring farms and villages. But the look of them, the associations, the buildings, the very materials from which the towns have got their texture through the centuries is different. In the tiny county of Rutland, Uppingham, on a hill, is a grey stone town of seventeenth and eighteenth century houses largely of one long main street: only a few miles away Oakham in the valley, the county town, is built mostly of plaster and brick, with several streets converging because, I suppose, in the great period of domestic building between one and two hundred years ago, stone was not so near Oakham as it was near Uppingham. I have found it useless to attempt anything but a selection of towns. And let it not be thought that these towns are 'typical': no English town is 'typical.' I have merely chosen small towns from different sorts of country. And even for different sorts of country I must make a qualification, There is no 'typical' English country. If you live in England you can tell by the colour, the contour, the people, the shapes of fields and churches and cottages whether you are in Devon or Somerset, in Lancashire or Cheshire. The counties are almost like separate countries, they differ so much in appearance: even parts of counties differ. The eight small towns, shortly noticed here, are not like all those near them; they have some resemblance to those in their neighbourhood, but they are not, in appearance, like one another.

Alnwick is a Northumberland fortress. It seems to have been built to resist the wind and the Scots; walls are thick; windows are small: stone and the winding river Aln guard you. This is a Celtic place: you would think it had as unwillingly submitted to Rome after the Synod of Whitby as submitted to the Crown after the Act of Uniformity. It is in a county of castles and few villages, except coal towns; the town does not fade gently into the country, as towns do in the softer south of England: you get the feeling you have come into a friendly enclosure after a long journey over bare hills, guided by the beacon turret of St. Michael's church. Once there were four gateways to the town, but now only one remains and the eighteenth century memorial of another. The Castle (Duke of Northumberland), still dominates the place, with a view down the Aln valley from its terraces and with a series of sumptuous rooms, some re-decorated when it was safe to lay out a park along the banks of the Aln and cultivated to adorn with Renaissance detail a mediaeval stronghold. From the town, a little more than a century ago, were issued beautiful little books for children illustrated with woodcuts in the manner of Bewick.

It was my delight in the varied worship in the Church of England that first brought me to Thaxted in Essex. For who had not heard of the late Conrad Noel, the Vicar who was called a Christian Communist and who hung the Red Flag in his church? Thaxted is as much a town as a large village, as are many of those half-towns, half-villages of East Anglia. Small hills, many elms, red tiled farms with cream or white plaster walls, little streams by which grow cricket-bat willows, and then the high stone spire of Thaxted church. Cottages and sedate brick houses form a broad street ending in a half timber hall on wooden stilts: a steep hill behind this and there is the huge fifteenth century church and behind it, the Georgian brick vicarage and a little cottage street sailing out into the country beyond. In the church sun streamed through great clear glass windows cutting across the blue waves of incense and the hanging banners of the chancel, in this white and living church: and with that renewed visual perception that comes after a church service when you are out in the world again, I saw, and have kept in my memory ever since, those prevailing summer colours of an East Anglian town—blue-black flint and grey lime-stone, orange-red tiles, dark green box hedges, dark red brick, and, gently spreading away below me, the pale-green elmy undulations of North Essex.

In Shropshire, the Severn winds down a valley

which is almost a gorge: deciduous woodland decorates its banks and here and there is a grassy clearing of parkland to reveal a country house, and round a bend is Bridgnorth, on a cliff above the rapid river. Of course there was a castle on such a site as this on the borders of Wales, but it is now an irregular fragment leaning over at a ridiculous angle and mocked by a municipal public garden around the masonry. Beneath on the Severn bank is the low town, brick houses with a hint of fishing about them and one hundred and eighty feet above is the High town with a twisting hill or a romantic cliff railway as the alternative ascent. Up here in the air, are two churches, one a classic design by Telford the great engineer and the other mediaeval. The main street of the High town is a mixture of inns, shops, black and white houses and pinkish brick, with a blacker and whiter Town Hall at one end of it. Ludlow, in the same county, is lovelier, it is probably the loveliest town in England with its hill of Georgian houses ascending from the river Terne to the great tower of the cross-shaped church, rising behind a classic market building. But Bridgnorth, especially if you come up by the little cliff railway, seems more rarified and remote, an Elizabethan dream approached by lift from the present century.

When I thought of the stone towns of middle England, a certain perverseness came over me, I would

LUDLOW, SHROPSHIRE

'probably the loveliest town in England.'

describe Highworth in North Wilts which no one visits
except to see relations and which has hardly an ugly
building in it, I would cut out the Cotswolds and
describe Oundle in Northampton or Rockingham or
Bloxham, all in districts which are like the Cotswolds
without their 'artiness.' But all the time the view of
Burford from the top of its hill, haunted me. Burford,
whose leaded windows look first on an avenue of pol-
larded limes and then across at one another as the hill
descends: Burford, the 'gem of the Cotswolds,' 'the
picturesque,' 'the quaint,' 'the Mecca of workers with
brush and pencil.' After all, it is only in the last fifty
years that Burford has been 'discovered' and the dis-
covery has preserved much of it from the speculator
and the improver. It is a town of golden stone in the
green-grey Cotswolds; a steep hill of mossy, stone-
roofed houses descending to the river Windrush; a
churchyard of baroque altar tombs of the seventeenth
and eighteenth centuries, a great wool church of the
last days of Christendom; a town of vistas through
Tudor openings on to stone hedges overrun with stone
crop and yellow wallflower: no one who has leant on
the bridge and looked down the little valley of the
Windrush and up at the climbing stone and the great
trees around the Priory can forget the inland peace of
such a town.

Chalk country breeds a colour of its own. Old red

brick takes on a warmer glow, limestone seems silver white, grass varies from gold to green on the swelling downs and beeches and elms have an eighteenth century look as though painted in by Gainsborough for a foreground or as distant globes of colour in an aquatint. So Blandford, seen from the hill on the road from Wiltshire into Dorset, glories in its brickwork, and chimney stacks are a landscape to themselves. Enter the town by back lanes to see the chimneys and the back gardens and soon you are out of the country into the wide Market place. This indeed is a handsome area. Blandford was burnt to the ground on June 4th, 1731, and two brothers named Bastard were employed in the re-building. They designed that handsome classic church of stone and the fountain before it, but they threw the shining ashlar of their church into contrast by building the larger houses in brick—I think I trace their hand in the sumptuous Crown Inn down by the River Stour and overlooking the beech-shaded park of Bryanston, and in one or two merchants' houses in the town. Blandford still looks like a scene in one of Wheatley's engravings, and perhaps its classic comeliness gave Alfred Stevens, who was born here, his taste for Renaissance. But it is an odd place to find the grave of Sam Cowell, the Cockney Victorian song writer and supposed author of 'The Ratcatcher's Daughter.'

In the West Country, in South Devon, the steep

BURFORD, OXFORDSHIRE, 1914

combes and luxuriant, fuchsia hedges remind the Irishman of Kerry, purple flowers of buddleia hang on walls, palms sprout among the chicken runs of farm-house gardens and high-banked lanes are luscious rockeries where gaps give a view of red earth and ash and oak and hazel hang over lanes. Maybe it is halluci-nation, but flowers and leaves in South Devon seem to grow larger than elsewhere in England. Towns are come on suddenly and I cannot do better than leave you to the description of one of them by William Allingham, the Irish poet, for the town has not much changed since he visited it about sixty years ago:

It was nightfall when I quitted the train at Totnes sta-tion, and walked off alone along a dark bit of road under the stars, to enter a strange town,—a special delight; turned a corner, into the long, narrow, roughly-paved High Street; downhill, to the poetic sign of The Seven Stars, a large, old-fashioned hostel, with garden to the river; then, after choosing bedroom, out again for the never-to-be-omitted-when-possible immediate and rapid survey, by any sort of light, of the place not seen before since I was born.

Up-hill goes the steep, narrow street, crossed, half way up, by a deep arch bearing a house; then the houses on each side jut on the side path supported on stumpy stone pillars; then I zig-zag to the left, still upwards, and by and by come to the last house, and the last lamp, throwing its gleam on the hedgerows and trees

46

of a solitary country road. This last house was an old and sizeable one, with mullioned windows, one of which is lighted, and on the blind falls a shadow from within of a woman sewing. The slight and placid movements of this figure, at once so shadowy and so real, so close at hand and so remote, are suggestive of rural contentment, a life of security and quietude. Yet how different from this the facts may be!

Next morning I mounted to the castle-keep of Judael de Totnais, through a wildly-tangled shrubbery, and from the mouldered battlements looked over Totnes's grey slate roofs and gables, and the silvery Dart winding amongst wooded hills. Opposite stood the tall, square, red sandstone tower of the old church, buttressed to the top, and with a secondary round turret running up from ground to sky near the centre of its north face, an unusual and picturesque feature. Then hied I to the churchyard, and beside it, in a rough back lane, saw an old low building, with an old low porch. The old key was in the old, iron-guarded door, and I entered, without question, the old Guildhall of the old town. Over the bench hung a board painted with the arms of Edward VI, supported by Lion and wyvern, 'Anno Domini 1553,' with motto, 'Du et mond Droyit.' The latticed windows looked into an orchard whose apples almost touched the panes. It was a little hall with a little dark gallery at one end, for the mediaeval public, and under this, the barred loopholes for the mediaeval parishioners to peep through.

Allingham is a little free with his use of 'mediaeval': more probably the court tried the early escapades at home of Elizabeth's Devon seamen!

# PORTS

THE SEA BREEDS A SPECIAL ARCHITECTURE IN England. All the old ports have rows of bow-windowed houses, generally Georgian, near the harbour or on heights overlooking the sea. To these merchant sea-men retire and spend their last days looking out through a telescope at the water. Brass front door knockers are highly polished, thresholds are scrubbed, reminders of clean decks and cabins, ships in bottles are suspended in parlours. Names like Nelson, William IV., Collingwood, Drake, Royal, Clarence, Arethusa, are commemorated by streets, columns, halls, public houses, hotels, victualling yards, docks. Nonconformist chapels abound and the more extreme forms of evangelicalism are to be found in churches of the Establishment. There are plenty of lodging houses for sailors and numerous missions to seamen, small front gardens have borders of cockle-shells and glittering lumps of quartz and here and there in a back garden or a yard you may find the huge wooden figurehead of a ship;

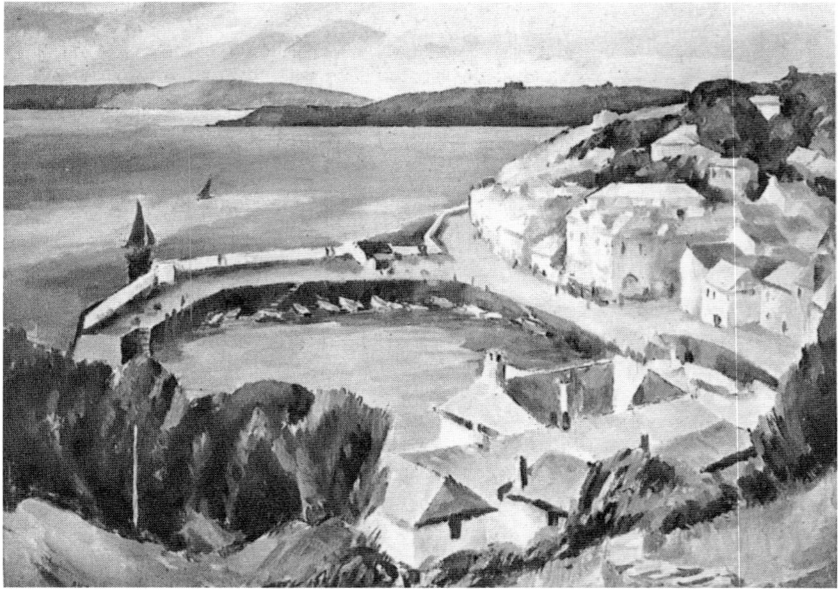

ST. MAWES, CORNWALL

there is a smell of tar, rope and salt in the air and weather vanes and flags among the houses tell everyone where the wind is blowing. These characteristics are common in English ports whatever their size. My mind reverts to Padstow, a tiny sea port on the estuary of the Camel in Cornwall—the feathery slate of old buildings round the quays, the narrow streets of slate houses climbing up to the church and the windy hills above, the marine store, the slate hung fronts of houses, the modest customs office, the black tarred warehouse, the smell of harbour mud at low tide and of salt and sea when dinghies are stirred on incoming water; the little streets where motor cars seem so unimportant after boats.

Nor is Liverpool, with all its extent of two-storey streets and polychrome hospitals and polytechnics, unattractive. Though St. George's Hall, that superbly proportioned example of the Greek period, is the finest public building in England, though the Walker Art Gallery has such a grand collection of Pre-Raphaelites, though the Cathedral looks so imposing at a distance (disappointing and unmysterious within), though the breezy Georgian terraces around the Cathedral and the Classic and restored Gothic churches in the city are among the best of their kind, still the soul of the place is around the six miles of docks. Here lead most of the roads to cobbled straight streets thundering with carts and lorries, flanked on the water side by enormous walls and guarded gateways, on the land side by bars, houses, shops and lodgings. The best way to see the docks is to take the overhead electric railway; Herculaneum, Brunswick, Coburg, Trafalgar, Queen's, Albert, Princess, Waterloo, Clarence, Collingwood, Nelson, Wellington, Huskisson, Canada, Alexandra—the names indicate the dates. Over the fogs and the levels of the Mersey, the cranes, the towers, the office blocks of Liverpool rise up, the most awe-inspiring port in England. The port of London may be larger, but Liverpool exists because it is a seaport town and as such it is a more attractive port than London.

Yet, to me, the best port of all is Bristol. There is no city in England with so much character. It keeps itself to itself. To Bristolians the Great Western Railway, which was inspired and largely financed by Bristol, is not a line for taking Bristolians to London, but for taking Londoners to Bristol, And, lest loyalty to Bristol should waver, there is on Paddington Station an advertisement of a Society of Bristolians in London. It is a town associated with rich men in the tobacco, wine and chocolate trades. Bristol is the capital of another kingdom, the West of England. From Bristol many of the social and religious movements of England have first received impetus. To this day a sturdy non-conformity governs the city—or rather the two cities.

One city is the port on the Avon, with narrow streets, old churches, half timber houses. It has a wooden eighteenth century theatre untouched since those days, with a pit where the stalls are in a modern auditorium. This was the port from which many ships sailed in Elizabeth's reign, when the masts of shipping stood up among the lace-like towers of churches, where it was still possible on a Sunday night before the war, when the bells were ringing for Evensong, to picture quaysides full of Elizabethan sailors. They seem to have left the air of the Spanish main, for in Bristol there are many wine vaults and the people drink wine at bars as they drink beer in other cities. My dear old friend, Canon W. L. Bowles of Brenthill and Salisbury, who died in 1850, has left a picture of Bristol in his poem *Banwell Hill* (1829):

> how proud,
> With all her spires and fanes, and volumed smoke,
> Trailing in columns to the midday sun,
> Black, or pale blue, above the cloudy haze,
> And the great stir of commerce, and the noise
> Of passing and repassing wains, and cars,
> And sledges, grating in their underpath,
> And trade's deep murmur, and a street of masts
> And pennants from all nations of the earth,
> Streaming below the houses, piled aloft,
> Hill above hill; and every road below

Gloomy with troops of coal nymphs, seated high
On their rough pads, in dingy dust serene: –
How proudly, amid sights and sounds like these,
Bristol, through all whose smoke, dark and aloof,
Stands Redcliff's solemn fane,— how proudly girt
With villages, and Clifton's airy rocks,
Bristol, the mistress of the Severn sea—
Bristol, amid her merchant-palaces,
That ancient city sits!

The eighteenth century stone houses climb up steep
hills past the beautiful and little-known Cathedral to
the second city, Clifton, another Bath, a late Georgian
spa on the heights of the Avon Gorge. The Gorge is
crossed by Brunel's Suspension Bridge, which is a delicate balanced structure, like an insect of enormous
size pausing astride the rocks and trees. And beyond
the Spa and the crowded port, stretch miles of solid
Victorian houses built of a pinkish sandstone, where at
the end of the road there is always a church, generally
Evangelical. Bristol has been bombed; much lace-like
carved stone of those Somerset towers and arcades has
been smashed, the delicate plasterwork (some of the
best in Europe) in Georgian houses has gone for ever:
yet Bristol seems much the same as when I last saw it.
The strong character is not destroyed nor have all its
best buildings and its narrow steep alleyways disappeared. Bristol will never die.

THE SEPHAMORE, PORTSMOUTH
Nineteenth-century engraving

BOSTON, LINCOLNSHIRE

From an engraving after J. M. W. Turner

So far all the ports I have described face west. Those which face south to France are, when they are of any size, on a comparatively low coast line. None has a finer setting than the three towns—Devonport, Stonehouse and Plymouth—looking over the sound to leafy Mt. Edgecumbe and the Cornish cliffs beyond.

None on the South coast had finer streets than these towns where marble pavements reflected, in the wet, nautical Georgian terraces and the whole colour of the town was the pale blue-grey of the local stone. Portsmouth, particularly the more ancient part close to the sea, had even more seventeenth century houses crowded near the water front; at Southsea naval officers retired and their daughters became engaged to young lieutenants at many a Southsea dance: and bars sold much pink gin.

The East coast ports are Dutch. Mellow brick houses have stepped battlements, the prevailing colours are from sand and brick. The old town of Harwich is the best of them, with its narrow streets on the peninsula between the Orwell and the Stour. In Lincolnshire, Boston might be a Dutch town out of which, unaccountably rises an enormous mediaeval church tower, Boston Stump, seen for miles across the fens and the sea.

Higher up in Yorkshire the moors jut into the sea and high cliffs take the place of sandy flats. Fishing villages have almost a Cornish look. Whitby lies where the river Esk forms a valley in the lias. The ruined Abbey looked down on the grey, narrow-streeted town and across the valley to a respectable collection of red-brick summer residences of the present century. Just below the Abbey stands the parish church, on a cliff. It is the least spoiled seaside church in the country. Dormer windows project from the roof, ancient pointed windows were fitted with wooden frames in the eighteenth century and they diversify lichen-covered walls. Within, is a forest of painted box pews, galleries stretch in all directions, even across the chancel screen. And the pews are lined inside with baize, some green, some blue, some pink. There seems never to have been enough room for the people of Whitby to hear a good sermon or to thank God for a good season. With so much joinery, you feel you are in the wooden hold of a ship.

AN EAST COAST FISH WHARF

Drawing by F. C. Jones

# INDUSTRIAL TOWNS

INDUSTRIAL TOWNS ARE ANOTHER SUBJECT. THEY should not be included in this book, which deals largely with the look of things—buildings first and people second. Except to connoisseurs of architecture, the industrial towns of England are more interesting for their people than for the buildings. From Mrs. Gaskell to D. H. Lawrence, from George Gissing to Arnold Bennett, the life of the industrial towns has been described intimately, and well. And since the larger proportion of our population is industrial, in the days of realistic writing that followed the last war, much English literature was about industrial towns. I could not, in a few paragraphs, describe the varieties of accent, habit and manners of the industrial districts of England whether Birmingham, Staffordshire, Durham, Cheshire or Lancashire. There is an individualism about industrial towns as great as that of country towns, but it is more a difference of population from population, than style of building from style of building.

A BUSY STREET IN LEEDS, 1890

The tram comes clicking through the suburbs, past the grand new Corporation building estate with its municipal gardens, big new school, shining brick church, wide grass and tree-planted verges. The road narrows somewhat as the larger villas begin, residences of former mayors, of managers and executives—all built before the last war. Each house has a garden and a carriage drive and over conifers and laurels may be seen the handsome residence, in the neo-Queen Anne, neo-Tudor or neo-Gothic style. From the top of the tram you look down on devotedly tended gardens, bright with begonias, to the sheltered tennis court and rustic summer-house. A bold Nonconformist church terminates an avenue and the tram enters the district of the older and still larger villas built, in the last century when the place was beginning to grow, for managers, mayors and aldermen. They are well proportioned buildings—the death knell of the old architectural traditions—in the Italian, Swiss or Grecian styles, rendered with stucco outside. But these are too big now for the sort of people who want to live as near to the town as this (it is nearly every Englishman's ambition to have enough money to live in the country), so the houses have been turned into flats and institutions and their gardens have the impersonal look that comes from corporate responsibility. Around some, the large garden has been built upon by speculators. And now the road is narrower still and the top of the tram is almost above the level of bedroom windows. We are on the hill above the valley wherein lies the centre of the town. The tram creaks down the curve, the little streets of red brick houses, climb up the hills all round; the vista of countless chimney pots is broken by a narrow Victorian spire. Terrace follows terrace in glazed brick, front doors by the hundred and then an arcade of little shops. A large Baptist Church, a larger Congregational Church, and larger still a Methodist Church: notices of mid-week services, a used looking church hall, pale green and brown glass in squares in the windows. The valley closes in on us, the river is crossed, black and flanked with factories, the great office buildings rise, whirling with terracotta decoration, the chain stores assert themselves with distinctive shop fronts, the huge emporium of the place glides by. Tram lines converge, public statues abound; buildings which might be termed the cathedrals of Baptists, Methodists, Unitarians, etc., prepare the way for a gigantic Town Hall built in the seventies or eighties. On another side of the square is the railway station and hotel in Early French Renaissance style. And beside the town hall is the great Library and Art Gallery (often with a large collection of pre-Raphaelites who were very popular with manufacturers, admirers of craftsmanship they could understand). These last buildings were probably the gift of a family since ennobled and living in a country house remote from the town which gave them the money to buy their social position. The high principled founder of the family fortune endowed his town with all that he missed in youth—the pictures, books, and a polytechnic—out of a mixture of affection for and conscience towards his native place.

Do not judge these industrial towns by their faces: they are the most alive places in England; they are more interesting than the little dead country towns which we so like to look at: think of Manchester and Birmingham with their concerts, theatres, parks, art galleries, cathedrals: notice the fine public buildings and Church of England churches of Leeds and Sheffield: the Town Hall at Huddersfield: the public buildings of Preston and Bradford. To someone who is not interested in people and social questions, the sight of the potteries at night or Bradford at night or of Manchester in one of its crimson smoky sunsets, is a sight never to be forgotten for beauty. To someone who likes people as well as buildings, the industrial towns are the hope and the life of England.

Market Street, Manchester.

MARKET STREET, MANCHESTER, 1907

THE QUEEN'S HOTEL, BRIGHTON, C. 1900

# SPAS AND WATERING PLACES

THE GREAT AGES OF TOWN BUILDING IN ENGLAND were the late eighteenth and early nineteenth centuries. There was a sense of planning, not of a single house, as there is to-day, and as there was before the eighteenth century, but of whole streets and towns. When the thermal water of Bath became popular in the eighteenth century, that small abbey town around the remains of a Roman Bath, spread stone terraces along the valley and hill. John Wood and his son were local architects and between them and their successor, Baldwin, they designed streets and crescents, Pump Room, Assembly Rooms, churches and chapels—all in a correct Palladian style, laid out to command views and vistas. Nowhere in Europe is there a more complete eighteenth century town than at Bath. The Nazi bombing has not destroyed its character, only obliterated for the time some of its details.

Bath is a stone town throughout. It climbs the North bank of the Avon. On a fine evening before the war you could watch the light on the great sweeps of Royal Crescent shadowy with attached columns; then the lights would come out in the S-shaped Lansdowne Crescent high on a hill, and in the blue valley would twinkle terraces and crescents of light as more lamps started up; you could hear the sheep grazing the grass before the Royal Crescent; you could lean on wrought iron railings and then walk down by narrow high walled alleys into the town and people the streets with sedan chairs and the main roads with coaches as the sun sank behind the high smooth hills.

Bath was mostly built between 1760 and 1810. It set a fashion for spas. Cheltenham, Gloucestershire, is the next most beautiful, a stuccoed town in the Regency manner, with lime and chestnut shaded pavements, sunny squares, classic terraces with delicate ironwork on verandahs and basement railings, single villas, now Swiss, now Gothic, now classic, and crescents and avenues, all in cheerful yellow stucco or golden Cotswold stone, shaded by trees and lightened with flowering shrubs. Papworth and Jearrard and Underwood were the chief architects of Cheltenham in the beginning of the last century. Here army and professional people retire to drink the chalybeate waters and frequent the circulating libraries.

Leamington, Warwick, is a similar town in stucco, slightly later and therefore less classic and more Gothic and Swiss in its plaster façades than Cheltenham but hardly less beautiful. There are large inland spas at Droitwich, Malvern, Harrogate and Tunbridge Wells, Woodhall and Buxton. But none of them have so much architectural merit as Bath, Cheltenham and Leamington. Clifton, which has ceased to be a spa, retains its early nineteenth century architecture.

After the visit of George III to Weymouth in the eighteenth century, watering places sprang up on the coast, and they must not be confused with the sea ports, where the sea is chastened by harbour bars and docks. In watering places, everything is a preparation for playing on the edge of the sea and for looking at it. Houses are more expensive, the better their view of the restless water. Little shrimping nets and wooden spades are for sale outside every stationer, bathing dresses dry on window sills, bathing machines diversify the beach, the pier, wriggling with whited ironwork, steps on slender iron legs into the waves.

Who can forget Brighton, the miles of stucco terraces, squares and crescents facing the English channel? On a silvery day the reflection of the sea on to white and yellow stone rising above wind-slashed veronica and tamarisk, lightens the heart and lifts up the rheumatic from his bath chair. Behind the terraces of Brighton are the 'lanes' of a fishing town and, in the centre of the place, George IV's sumptuous Oriental

Pavilion rears light domes and minarets of plaster. Less spoiled and smaller than Brighton are St. Leonard's, Dover, Ramsgate and Margate built in the same spacious late-Georgian time. On the North coast are Tynemouth, Scarborough and Cromer in the same style. In the West Country, Weymouth, Lyme Regis, Torquay, Dawlish, Teignmouth, Sidmouth—each watering place reflecting the character of its county.

After watering places come seaside places; which are of a later age, less planned, less beautiful than the Georgian and early Victorian watering places, built in an age when detached houses were popular and the notion was current that an Englishman's home was his castle, even if it was only a windy bungalow hired for the summer months. Sometimes these seaside resorts grew round a decayed fishing port where there was a beach or where a speculator had built one handsome terrace as for a watering place which never caught on or where the subsoil was recommended by the medical profession, or the sands were wide. The chief are Bournemouth, Newquay, Skegness, Eastbourne, Weston-super-Mare, Frinton, Blackpool, Bridlington. Expensive hotels and even more expensive houses face the sea and the front, with sea shrubs in the garden, bronzed people eating ices in deck chairs, slot machines clicking and Edwardian kiosks selling rock and local views. Behind the houses on the sea front run roads at right angles where the lodgings are slightly cheaper. These roads lead to the shopping street, running parallel with the sea front off which are places of worship for every variety of churchmanship and sect; behind them are the cheapest lodgings of all. On the inland edge of the town is a park for those permanent residents who have to live in the town all the winter when the wind makes the seafront impossible. Villas of all colours and styles edge the skyline: they make a London suburb by the sea, but a suburb with exquisite country within walking distance.

THE BOAT LANDING AND PROMENADE, BLACKPOOL.
Lithograph from *An Album of Blackpool Views*

# HOW TOWNS GREW AND HOW THEY WILL GROW

WHAT THE QUARRIES HAVE DONE FOR THE COLOUR of English towns, transport has done for their plan and shape. Many may be said to have stayed put, fishing towns round a natural harbour, ports on a navigable river, strips of houses by coal mines or around factories whose existence depends on their proximity to coal or upon some product of the earth on which they stand. These towns, though many of them are large and little visited by the uncommercial, can never move or expand far outwards or wane except that their industry cease to be essential—because the source from which their inhabitants derive their existence is immovable. Such towns do not expand in the way most English towns expand.

The average inland English town owes its importance to the transport which reaches it. When roads were shocking, and cattle were driven along hill tops: when valley people knew nothing of those who lived in the next valley: when as Hardy noticed fifty years ago, autumn thistledown and butterflies flew from the meadows at one end of High Street to the cornfield at the other without noticing that the country town between was not a field, so closely identified was it with country life—England was pitted with small towns, the most convenient centres for a number of villages. And these were large or small according to the number of their surrounding farms. Maybe there were other reasons for a town's existence—a prosperous religious establishment, a position at a ford, or bridge, or in a sheltered valley. But it is noticeable to-day that the old towns of agricultural England are approached by many little lanes. When the town has grown, these little lanes have become the streets of small suburbs. These devious ways were for the convenience of farm carts and drovers. The town dwellers themselves and the carters and drovers, once they had reached the market place, had no further need of a wheeled vehicle during the day. So houses are islanded among passages, paths for walkers only, leading to church and green, the two most used places in early days.

Until roads improved, towns remained very much the same in size, only increasing or decreasing with the birthrate and another county was almost another country.

By the eighteenth century coaching had opened up one county to another. Though the repairs of roads was still chargeable to parishes, the main coaching roads of England brought additional prosperity to the towns and turnpike fees kept the roads in repair. Inns were large as Town Halls, with spreading stables behind. Fortunate was the town which was situated at a convenient coaching stage on the road to Scotland or Bath or Weymouth or the Midlands or the West: then rose the handsome houses with balconies on the first floor windows to watch the elegant vehicles rattle past. Coloured prints of such scenes (generally fakes) hang in the halls and lounges of most English hotels.

A country town in those days became accessible and many an owner of a country house would buy or rent a mansion in the country town and many an apothecary, lawyer and merchant would build a town house, out of the money made from all the county folk coming to the country town for the season.

Coaching roads and the coaches caused the people of the richer sort to live in country towns for the season. By the end of the eighteenth century the canals brought the bricks for whole terraces of new houses. Meanwhile the centre of the town remained the market square; there was the big hotel and there came farm carts from the villages to market and the droves of cattle as they always had come. Land value in the centre of the town went up, so the plan remained the same.

The great change came with the railways.

Thereafter the centre of business shifted to the neighbourhood of the railway station. The market square became less important than the goods yard. The old inn decayed and the smart new railway hotel with its gas light and billiards saloon drew the commercials and the Victorian business men. Clumps of houses gathered round the railway and if the size of the town demanded it, a suburban station was built a mile or two away and around this arose respectable residences for the semi-prosperous. Some towns, especially old country towns whose mayor and council preferred the horse to the steam engine, refused to co-operate with the railways. When they learned the line was coming, they refused to let it near the town: they foresaw the decay of the market square where their capital was invested, where they had met in the smell of straw and livestock for generations So a station was built some miles from the town and the town itself decayed because the townsmen were unwilling to use the transport which would bring them prosperity. Thus it is you will find all over England branch lines built at a later date than the main line, going to old country towns, sad little tracks of single line winding through meadowland and valley to an imposing but nearly deserted terminus. Sometimes it happened that the railways, once their position was secure, refused to go out of their way to bring the line to a small town. Sometimes the citizens themselves, in

LONDON & GREENWICH RAILWAY, 1836
'The great change came with the railways.'

remorse, constructed a line of their own. The railway increased the size of some towns. Elsewhere it created new ones—Crewe, Swindon, Wolverton and Redhill. But the limitation of the railway was the places where it could stop. The more trains stopped at a town the greater became its commercial importance. Any town with a frequent service of trains became densely populated. We are inclined to blame the Victorians for the planlessness of industrial towns, for thin strips of two storey streets, that line either side of the railway line. But until trams and bicycles came into existence it was not practicable for people working in a factory to live on the outskirts of a mid-Victorian industrial town.

The density created at certain places by the railways has been thinned out by the motor car. For whereas a goods train and a passenger train has a prescribed stopping place on the line, lorries or private cars can stop anywhere along a road. They can start at any time and stop at any place. There is no trouble with waiting at junctions, with changing from one line to another. The motor lorry, by providing a cheap, rapid method of transport altered the plan of most of the English towns. Light industry, that is to say industry which is not confined to a certain district, has moved from the congested towns of the North of England and the Midlands, to main roads outside London and the big ports, or to the outskirts of the town whose centre it originally occupied. Stretches of pylons and forests of poles have brought electric power out to the country so that it is possible for a factory to be built on almost any site. Where is it more natural to build a modern factory than beside a main road? For here is a broad route, provided by the State, for lorries which can leave the factory at any time for any destination. Buses and private cars can bring visitors from far greater distances than in the constricted days of railways. The sons of the silk-hatted first-class travellers and even those of the second-class travellers on the old steam trains, could buy private cars before this war. They all have the Englishman's love of the country. In their new-found freedom they used to rush to the country and crowded every accessible town and village with clusters of semi-rural communities extending over a greater area by far than that occupied by the original town. Speculative builders, eager to save themselves the expense of building roads and drains and bringing power to country districts, built villas along the main roads where surface and light and drainage and power were already available. So the roads came into their own again and ribbon development, that most natural development, was the direct result of the motor car. Transport determined the plan and towns spread outwards until they nearly touched one another. Coaching towns on main roads came once more into their own.

The old inn in the market square was taken over by a combine and re-furbished in a half-timber style, vaguely reminiscent of a few hundred years before it was built: the stable became a garage: the market square became a car park; tea rooms opened in the main street; the old shop fronts disappeared as lorries brought the mass-produced shop fittings, advertisements, films, signs, petrol pumps, magazines, multiple stores, the Morris's, Fords, Daimlers, buses and chars-à-banc brought the people. On first glance, many towns came to look like a London suburb.

The Railway Hotel remained gas-lit and unused as an overflow for people who could not get in to the old-new coaching inn. Grass grew in the sidings of the branch railway. Finally the line was closed to passenger traffic. The cars, lorries and the luxury coaches roared over the tarmac.

The future of small towns, county towns, cathedral towns, seaports and watering places and spas was insecure. In England, people respect natural scenery and they respect buildings which are manifestly 'old' even if they are sham-antique. Generations of guide book writers have been antiquaries interested only in what is pre-Reformation and sometimes, greatly daring, admiring the early work of the Renaissance. But the buildings of the late eighteenth and early nineteenth centuries, those modest brick and stone houses, simple

The Omnibus

'Buses and private cars can bring visitors from far greater
distances than in the constricted days of railways.'

town halls, elegant bridges, terraces and crescents and squares, without which almost every old English town would lose all its texture and proportion, and become as desolate as a bombed area—these relics of the greatest age of domestic building are ignored, partly because they are so reticent, so unobtrusively effective and partly because they are not regarded as ancient. Many original Victorian churches and public buildings are equally ignored. And in reaction from this admiration for the ancient, there has grown up an absurd admiration of what is modern, as though 'modern' meant always a flat roof, a window at the corner, the construction of concrete and steel, imitated in brick; wallpaper designed in cubes and darts of orange and brown; no capital letters, and no serifs on shop fascias; horizontal glazing bars— in fact not genuine contemporary architecture at all but 'jazz.' This jazz-modern fashion produced as many enormities as the craze for sham Elizabethan. I see it developing beyond individual buildings into easy generalisation about the new world after this war, into silly assumption that everything old must be pulled down and we must all live in skyscrapers made of glass and steel and worthy of the new age for which we fight. Heaven forbid that we are fighting for such textureless materialism. While Ludlow stands, while Burford High Street rises from the Windrush, while the spas and watering places of

QUEENSTOWN BRIDGE, SWINDON, 1885
Oil painting by G. Puckey

THE GREAT NORTH ROAD AT CASTLEFORD, SOUTH YORKSHIRE

England stretch crescents and terraces, however old and blasted, to the hills or to the sea, we have an England to protect. Let us rebuild the grey industrial towns where August is unbearable and where the country is out of reach, but let us leave the rest of England alone.

Before the war we stood by and watched an ignorant local councillor or a greedy speculator in housing, ruin the appearance of a whole street by one building of the wrong material; the wrong proportion and the wrong texture and the wrong colour. There were vague bye-laws, earnest local preservation societies and a singular planlessness about local planning.

But the war has given us a double hope. Nazi bombing has built up an affection for the old towns of England among those many who formerly thought little about them: the need for communal effort in so many things has galvanised us into activity. There is at last, what has been wanted for the last fifty years, a Ministry of Works and Buildings which will, I believe, preserve the old cities and towns of Britain by allowing for future building development on a national scale and along natural lines; transport will no longer be considered as secondary; conflicting local bye-laws will be adjusted. The old system of building a new suburb first and letting modern transport come along later, will be abolished.

We have seen in this chapter how the transport has

determined the shape of every English town, since English towns began. To-day, a lorry, a bus, or a private car can cross England over-night therefore the whole of England becomes the subject for planning, not a single county, still less a single town. Much rubbish about 'opening up vistas,' 'rural slums,' 'post war reconstruction,' has been appearing in the press: but there is no doubt that only by planning on a national scale will we preserve the hundreds of beautiful old cities of England.

> For time has softened what was harsh when new
> And now the stones are all of sober hue.

These old towns of England are numerous enough to survive a decade of barbarian bombing. But their texture is so delicate that a single year of over enthusiastic 'post war reconstruction' may destroy the lot. Because so many more English people have grown aware of how beautiful are her old cities and towns and because of the hope we place in a national plan to preserve them, these pages and pictures will, please God, serve as a guide to future visitors and not survive as a sad memorial volume.

John Betjeman 1943

# APPENDIX

D O NOT JUDGE A TOWN BY ITS ANTIQUITIES ALONE as do the guide books, nor a town by its pubs, as do the motorists.

Judge it instead by everything you see in it, the new as well as the old, the people as well as the bricks and stay in it and study it with the same reverence that you would study the towns in Italy. Only by so doing will Casterbridge open itself and will Barchester reveal its sequences of architecture and even the Five Towns become a place of pilgrimage.

I give below a list of the dates of various buildings to be found in a town. Since there are few mediaeval, compared with other buildings in most English towns, I have devoted less space to them than the antiquary would desire and more space to the quantity of eighteenth, nineteenth, and twentieth century buildings which make a town.

*Norman (Romanesque), Religious, Secular, c.1050–c.1200*

Round arches, and thick unbuttressed walls in parish churches, a door or an arcade or font. A castle (almost in ruins). A castle mound. A town wall, barbican.

*Gothic (Early English and Decorated), c.1250–c.1350*

Some feature of the parish church. A ruined abbey or priory. Additions to castle or walls.

*Gothic (Perpendicular), c.1400–c.1500*

Most of the church. Town churches were generally re-built in these prosperous times of the middle ages. Market Cross, a small chapel of ease.

*Early Seventeenth Century, 1600–1650*

Almshouses, timber part of an inn, a brick or stone house, rarely more than two storeys high, with brick or stone hood moulds for the windows and a stone bar dividing the window opening into oblong spaces of leaded panes: ancient Grammar Schools.

*Late Seventeenth Century, 1650–1699*

Timber cottages: brick houses and stone ones with steep gables and windows as described in paragraph above: almshouses; small and ancient-looking public houses, approached by steps down from the level of the street.

*Early Eighteenth Century, 1700–1750*

Brick or stone houses, three or four storeys high with carved central doors, long narrow windows with thick wooden bars framing small panes, a parapet along

MARKET CROSS, MALMESBURY

Water colour by Frances Macdonald

the top hiding the roof. Unitarian, Quaker, Baptist and Congregational places of worship. Larger inns, possibly a custom house in seaport towns or town hall.

*Late Eighteenth Century,* 1750–1799

Large coaching towns: town halls, tall houses with ironwork outside, pillared portico, large windows, largest on ground or first floor, getting smaller in ascending stories. Thinner wooden glazing bars, forming larger and more oblong shaped panes than those mentioned in the last paragraph. Bow-windowed shop fronts; wharves and warehouses of ancient appearance: sometimes whole crescents and terraces of houses. Semi-circular fanlights over front doors, leadwork in varying patterns came in at the end of the century. The earliest Methodist chapels.

*Early Nineteenth Century*, 1800–1839

Oblong-paned shop-fronts, sometimes in bow-window form; plain stucco facades affixed to seventeenth century buildings to bring them in line with neighbours, terraces, crescents and squares, plain exteriors whose effect is gained by the proportion of window to wall space: detached stucco villas, plain or Greek, on the outskirts of towns; canal wharves, quays and locks and bridges; assize courts, Methodist and Congregational chapels, built or restored in the Greek manner, mostly in plaster or local stone; new streets, generally broad and straight; in High Street a row of shops belonging to different firms, but made to harmonise in one scheme: great town halls and covered markets: one or two imitation Tudor villas, generally built in stucco. Trees planted in open spaces where possible, particularly beeches, copper beeches and pseudo-acacias, elms and limes.

*Church and Chartist period*, 1840–1869

Preliminary 'restoration' of parish churches, introduction of plate glass into shop fronts and removal of old glazing bars in windows (ruining the proportions of their exteriors), the inserting of plate glass instead; rebuilding of older Non conformist churches in Italianate and Decorated styles. Private banks, particularly Savings Banks; early railway stations, generally of local stone and in Swiss, Tudor or Italianate styles: large gardens of eighteenth and early nineteenth century town houses built over with small plain cottages forming courts and alleys at rear of main streets, generally in brick. One or two large merchants' houses in Italian, Tudor or Swiss styles in suburbs. Chapels of ease, suburban churches in stone with spires in Decorated or Early English style. Front gardens of older houses in streets which have become commercial, built over so as to form shops. Corn Exchanges.

*Late Nineteenth Century*, 1870–1899

Further restoration of parish church; rebuilding of older chapels in Decorated, Early English and

Perpendicular styles (in brick with terracotta dressings). Great use of brick, generally red or glazed, for all secular work. Fire Station, Post Office, Public Library, Salvation Army and Mission Halls: railway stations, suburban stations; streets of bow-fronted, two-storey red brick villas, in terrace form or semi-detached, in neighbourhood of station, very small front gardens with iron fence and low wall and small back garden, these villas sometimes diversified with white brick; red or brown terracotta frontages to banks, institutions and shops; exclusive villas on outskirts in brick, Gothic or a baroque-ish Queen Anne with plum-coloured gables and wooden balconies, also painted plum, green or white. Red ridge tiles to slate roofs. Drinking fountains and jubilee clock towers.

*Twentieth Century, pre-Great War,* 1900–1914

Town Halls and Public Libraries built of glazed brick in a Jacobean style, roofs of villas given bright red tiles; banks and shops rebuilt in solid Jacobean style; suburbs of detached houses formed, the houses with bright red roofs, gables, French windows on ground floor, white wooden balconies; laburnum, pink maybe, behind ornate wooden fences. Arcades of shops built near railway stations; piers, shelters at seaside towns ; cottage hospitals; recreation grounds and small public parks: shelters, bandstands and kiosks and refreshment rooms; privet hedges and flowering shrubs in parks;

GREAT SHAMBLES, YORK
Water colour by Michael Rothenstein

one or two 'artistic' villas, pebble dashed, small windows, sloping buttresses, black-tarred chimney stacks, hygienic looking, belonging to doctors and lawyers who have left centre of town: Elementary Schools.

*Twentieth Century. Mid-War period*, 1918–1938

Earlier part of period characterised by quantity of imitation half-timbering added to eighteenth century inns; gables of modern villas, proportions of villas different by reason of standard-size windows mass-produced in wood or steel; whole character of main streets altered by shop fronts of multiple stores with regulation fascia in every town: shop windows enlarged to take up half the first floor of the old houses in which they are set; a great deal of demolition of unpretentious building of previous two centuries and over-furbishing up of 'mediaeval' buildings. Banks and Municipal Buildings in a refined Georgian style, generally out of proportion with the rest of the street. Council Housing Estates on outskirts of town, varying in style according to the lack of sensibility of local councils. Large Hospitals. Bungalows on outskirts; red roofs; main motor roads lined with two-storey, semi-detached villas with large front gardens, rockeries, sham half-timber gables; stained glass front doors, chains along garden walls, wooden gates, wooden garages. Garages and tin signs and hoardings on all main roads. Cinemas, very often in a 'modern' style, as may be one or two villas—not really modern, but jazz; bricks at this time were of a less bright shade of red than earlier in the century. Houses no longer built in terraces, semi-detached or detached and a good way apart, by reason of the Town Planning Acts. Schools.

There are two rules which may form a useful addendum for people on the look out for old buildings. But as they are generalisations they cannot be guaranteed accurate in all cases.

1. *How to tell an old roof from a modern one*. Tiles of uniform size, except in certain parts of East Anglia, Middlesex and Kent and Yorkshire, were not used until well on into the nineteenth century. Stone roofs and slate roofs until about 1850 were always built with their tiles graded from small at the ridge getting gradually larger towards the eaves.

2. *How to tell old bricks, stone and half timber* from the modern equivalent. Use your eyes. Old things are mellow and worn, new things hard and sharp whether brick, stone or wood. Old walls, especially in churches and old brick houses, have been despoiled of their texture by 'snail pointing' with grey cement – that is to say the divisions between the stones and bricks have been emphasised by hard straight lines made with a trowel.

HALIFAX FROM BEACON HILL.
Lithograph from Pearson's
*Royal Cabinet Album of Halifax*

*colour plates*

The Boston May Sheep Fair, 1830

Thaxted, Essex, The Manor Hall

The Cathedral, Chester

The Cathedral at Canterbury, Kent, 1887

Market Street, Manchester, 1907

The Queen's Hotel, Brighton, *c.* 1900

Queenstown Bridge, Swindon, 1885
-Oil painting by G. Puckey

The Great North Road at Castleford,
South Yorkshire -Water colour by F.C. Jones, 1946

*black & white*
*illustrations*

South Gate Street, Leicester
Family in a railway compartment
The Hen and Chickens Hotel, Birmingham
Hancock's Glass Shop, Birmingham
Newbury, Berkshire, 1920
Pub in Canning Town
Wye Bridge and Cathedral, Hereford
The Peace Festival at Salisbury, 1856
Ely Cathedral
Houses at Oxford
King's College Chapel, Cambridge
Ludlow, Shropshire
Burford, Oxfordshire, 1914
St. Mawes, Cornwall
The Sephamore, Portsmouth
Boston, Lincolnshire
An East Coast Fish Wharf
A Busy Street in Leeds, 1890
The Boat Landing and Promenade, Blackpool

London & Greenwich Railway, 1836
The Omnibus
Market Cross, Malmesbury
Great Shambles, York
Halifax from Beacon Hill

# Acknowledgments

PRION HAVE ENDEAVOURED TO OBSERVE THE LEGAL requirements with regard to the rights of suppliers of illustrative material and would like to thank Mary Evans Picture Library for their generous assistance.